Peter and Wendy

Growing Up in Neverland

Dennis J. Billy, CSsR

En Route Books and Media, LLC
St. Louis, MO

⊕*ENROUTE*
Make the time

En Route Books and Media, LLC
5705 Rhodes Avenue
St. Louis, MO 63109

Cover credit: Sebastian Mahfood

ISBN-13: 978-1-952464-93-5
Library of Congress Control Number: 2021943391

Dedication

To Michael, Richard, and Laura,
who explored the Neverland with me.

"Wendy, Wendy, when you are sleeping in your silly bed you might be flying about with me saying funny things to the stars."

~Peter Pan

Contents

Introduction 1

Poem: Peter 9

Chapter One: Life at Home 11

Chapter Two: An Inner World 17

Chapter Three: Losing Your Shadow 23

Chapter Four: Coming and Going 31

Chapter Five: Round and Round 39

Chapter Six: Building and Playing House 47

Chapter Seven: The Mermaid's Lagoon 55

Chapter Eight: The Never Bird 63

Chapter Nine: The Happy Home 71

Chapter Ten: Wendy's Story 79

Chapter Eleven: Carried Off 87

Chapter Twelve: Believing in Fairies 93

Chapter Thirteen: The Pirate Ship 99

Chapter Fourteen: Hook or Me 107

Chapter Fifteen: The Return Home 115

Chapter Sixteen: When Wendy Grows Up 123

Poem: Wendy 133

Introduction

This book looks at J. M. Barrie's classic children's story *Peter Pan*[1] to see what it can tell us about ourselves and our situation today. It discovers in this classic fairy-tale about the boy from Neverland who refuses to grow up an extensive map of a child's mind and the painful process of becoming an adult. Fairy tales are "literary dreams," if you will, that reveal to the reader the intricate workings of the human psyche. They use images and symbols to manifest both the deepest hopes and the greatest fears of the human heart. As such, they enable us to experience on a conscious level the forces at work deep in the realm of our unconscious lives. *Peter*

---

[1] *Peter Pan* first appeared on the British stage in 1904. For literary purposes, the book follows the version of the tale that was published by Barrie in novel form under the title *Peter and Wendy* in 1911 and as *Peter Pan and Wendy* in 1921 All quotations in this book come from a recent reprint of this novel version of the story: J. M. Barrie, *Peter Pan* (New York: Bantam Classic, 1985).

Pan is no exception. From the moment it first appeared on the British stage, it has given its readers a penetrating (albeit fleeting) glimpse into the complex makeup of the human mind.

For more than one hundred years, Barrie's masterpiece has fascinated audiences throughout the world. The reason for its success is its ability to strike a sensitive chord deep within the human psyche. When we read it, the tale unlocks the powers of the imagination, enabling us to peer into the dark well of human consciousness and experience firsthand the underlying psychological forces at work in us. Through it, we experience the danger and risk, the joy and excitement, the innocence and sadness of a child's complex journey to adulthood.

The story appeals to readers of all ages (a mark of great literature) and invites them to enter into it on their own terms. Children are able to recognize in it many of the tensions, fears, and hopes that they go through in the initial stages of their adventurous walk through life. Middle-aged adults are invited to recall and get back in touch with the children they once were and, to a large extent, still remain. The elderly read it with the eyes of that second childhood that accompanies them through their later stages of life. Anyone who takes the time to absorb it and allow its imagery to speak to the heart can benefit from its message. How could it be otherwise? The story offers its readers an opportunity to step back and take a good hard look at the strong psychological forces at work in their lives from the earliest moments of their existence. It is a vehicle for self-understanding, the simplicity of which is equaled only by its sensitive and probing insights into a child's world and the various complicating factors that go into changing it.

The book is divided into sixteen chapters. Each contains a brief exposition of the plot, followed by some observations about the story's deeper meaning and a series of reflection questions designed to assist the reader in drawing out the implications for his or her life. The purpose of this format is to present the story in as clear and as straightforward a way as possible while giving the reader ample opportunity to look beneath the surface of the story to find its personal relevance for his or her life. In this way, the reader finds plot, narrative interpretation, and opportunities for personal reflection in close proximity to each other, a helpful arrangement for innovative and fruitful thought.

The chapters as a whole are situated between two poetically arranged prose pieces from Barrie's classic tale. The first, entitled *Peter*, paints a portrait of the adventurous boy from Neverland whose exploits we follow throughout the tale. The second, entitled *Wendy*, does the same for the story's heroine and serves to remind us that the tale really is all about a child's struggles with growing up rather than a refusal to do so. These poetic passages incite the imagination and remind us of the choice each of us must sooner or later make about our attitude toward childhood in our adult lives. As such, they serve as suitable bookends for what the reader finds between the book's covers.

This book is not meant to replace the fairy-tale, but to complement it. It recognizes that nothing can take the place of a thorough, firsthand knowledge of the text itself. For this reason, it encourages the reader to delve into the original at his or her convenience in order to savor the many nuances that the brief expositions of the plot contained in the present book can hardly do justice to. The purpose of this book, one might say, is "to break open" the tale and make its rich inner meaning available to a wider audience. It is a "commentary," of sorts, that challenges the reader to reassess what he or she might otherwise write off all too easily as a mere child's tale with little to offer by way of serious reflection on the meaning of human existence. What a mistake it would be to come to such a conclusion. What a triumph it would be if this book were to help even a small handful of interested readers to recognize *Peter Pan* for the literary gem that it is and for the deep font of wisdom it contains.

The tale, of course, is not without its limitations. Written in the early years of the 1900s, it reflects many of the values of late-colonial Britain such as unconditional loyalty to the king, belief in Rule Britannia, and the ideal of the English gentleman. It also perpetuates a number of culturally conditioned stereotypes, many of which have long since changed or proved to be inadequate (e.g., describing Indians as savages; using a term such as "gay" to describe a "happy" child). As one might expect, the makeup of the Darling household reflects more the customs and values of turn of the century middle-class British society than the less rigid, non-nuclear family units so common in America today. The reader must be patient when coming across such peculiarities and make appropriate adaptations along the way. Otherwise, he or she will fail to see its deeper message and be easily disappointed. Every story is historically conditioned; *Peter Pan* is no exception. Not all tales, however, have relevance beyond the historical climate from which they come. Barrie's tale has it because of its unique capacity to tap the deep well of the human psyche and display its contents before our eyes in an imaginative, narrative shape. It would be a shame if the tale's subtle prejudices and petty biases were to get in the way of its deeper, universal relevance to the human situation.

The insights offered in this book in no way exhaust the meaning of the tale. They seek only to be the beginning of a much deeper and wider reflection that the reader will carry out on his or her own. For this reason, the reader would be well-advised to go through the book slowly and put it aside when serious questions that it does not address arise and persist in his or her mind. It would be much more worthwhile to pursue that line of thinking rather than sticking slavishly to the questions raised in the text simply because they are there. When seen in this light, the book seeks to be a touchstone for serious, sustained reflection on an individual's journey to human maturity. It will raise questions about a person's fear of growing up, ask if those fears have ever been confronted (let alone resolved), and look for an honest reassessment of a person's childhood memories. It will go a long way in helping a person come to terms with the issues of his or her "lost childhood" and should be of great help to the various audiences mentioned above. Every book has its limits and this one is no exception. As a point of departure for further reflection, its own perceptions and intuitions can only go so far. At some point, the reader must take responsibility for the process that has been initiated and see it to its proper end. Otherwise, the book will fail in its purpose of sparking serious reflection on the psychological forces uncovered by Barrie's masterful tale.

One final observation needs mentioning. This book says very little about God but is very much about God. Coming to a deeper knowledge of oneself prepares a person for a deeper knowledge of the creator. This is so not because the human and the divine are one and the same, but because one is a reflection, a veritable image, of the other. As *imago Dei*, the human person images God in a way that no other living being is capable. Barrie's tale is not overtly religious and was never meant to be. It reveals, however, that which is genuinely human and, as such, offers its readers the possibility of experiencing the divine (be it ever so faintly) in the reverberating echoes rising from deep within the human heart. When a person becomes more fully aware of himself or herself, intimacy with the divine is always a real possibility. Self-knowledge is both a gift and a prerequisite for knowledge of the divine. Whenever and wherever it occurs, the presence of the divine is rarely far away.

Peter[2]

Then
Peter
knew
that there
was not
a moment
to lose.

"Come,"
he cried
imperiously,
and soared out
at once
into the night,
followed
by John
and Michael
and Wendy.

Mr. and Mrs. Darling
and Nana
rushed
into the nursery
too late.

The birds were flown.

---

[2] Barrie, *Peter Pan*, 35. [Poetically arranged]

Chapter One

Life at Home

Peter Pan is very much a tale about growing up. This comes across most clearly in the novel version of the story, which first appeared in 1911 under the title *Peter and Wendy* and which begins with the line: "All children, except one, grow up." Peter, of course, is the exception; Wendy, the rule. She shares top billing with Peter because the story is just as much about her journey from childhood to adulthood as it is about Peter's exploits with the lost boys in the fantasy world of Neverland—perhaps more. Wendy represents all children who one day will become adults and all adults who one day were children. From the beginning of the story to its end, the reader enters into her character and identifies with it more than any of the others. As a result, the reader grows with Wendy and, like her, is able to embrace the Neverland as the story unfolds and let it go at the appropriate time.

The Darling Household

To understand Wendy, one must first understand the home she comes from. Mrs. Darling, her mother (we never learn her first name), is a lovely, romantic woman whose sweet mocking mouth always withholds a kiss that can never quite be captured. She has vague memories of Neverland from her own childhood and once even believed in Peter Pan herself. But that was long, long ago. Now, she keeps busy running the Darling household and tidying up her children's minds. She loves to have everything in its place, although she has been known to slip up on her books and, at times, misplace whole cauliflowers with pictures of babies without faces.

George Darling, Wendy's father, is a conscientious, good-hearted, but calculating man. He wins his wife's hand by taking a cab and popping the question first, while her other suitors raced to her door by foot. He figures all the numbers out ahead of time and likes to cut corners in his expenses. When Wendy is born, he makes extensive calculations to see if he and his wife have the means to keep her. He does the same at the birth of his sons,

John and Michael. He also hires a prim Newfoundland called Nana as his children's Nanny. Although he is concerned about what others might say about placing a dog in such an important post, he feels certain that his children will receive the best possible care—and he is right.

Nana takes exceptional care of the children and is loved by all the family (although Mr. Darling suspects she does not admire him). All things considered, the Darling family is quite content—at least, until Peter Pan comes upon the scene. It is not uncommon for them to break out into dance and wild pirouettes. At such times, even little Liza the maid, the only other servant in the Darling household, would join in their happy frolicking.

Looking Deeper

Wendy belongs to an admittedly strange, but unusually happy family. Her mother is a romantic; her father, a good-natured but worrying cheapskate. She has a dog for a nanny and a midget for a maid.

At first sight, it seems as though the only normal people in the entire household are the three Darling children. That may well be so, but the reader must remember that Wendy, John, and Michael are the heroes of the story (especially Wendy) and that the author has taken great pains to portray their family life as they would have experienced it. Mrs. Darling represents feminine charm and beauty; Mr. Darling, the practical and calculating masculine mind. Nana stands for the instinctual dimension of their family household which is kept under tight reins by her master. Liza, the least developed character of the lot, represents the functional dimension of the household, which executes orders grudgingly but without protest.

The inner workings of the Darling household convey a sense of creative chaos. All decisions are thoroughly thought-out but seem strangely irrational and out of place. With such unusual inner family dynamics, one has to wonder how the Darlings get by on a daily basis, let alone thrive. But, somehow, they do. Wendy and her brothers come from a quirky, but loving home. They feel wanted, secure, and very much at home in their home, so much so that one has to wonder why they would ever want to leave it.

Reflection Questions

1. What are your earliest memories of your family?
    How would you describe your mother? Your
    father? Your brothers and sisters, if you had
    any? What are your fondest memories of your
    early family life? What are your most painful
    memories of it?

2. How would you describe the inner dynamics of
    your early family life? How did your family
    members relate? How did you relate to them?
    How were the roles assigned? Were they per-
    formed well? Poorly? Were your family dyna-
    mics dysfunctional in any way?

3. How did reason and affection, instinct and func-
    tion interact in your early family life? Were
    some valued more than others? Did some family
    members appropriate some to the exclusion of
    others? If so, which ones? Did you ever appro-
    priate any to yourself?

4. Did you feel loved and secure in your early
    family life? Or did you feel afraid, unwanted,
    and abused? Do you now feel a little of both? If
    so, does one feeling predominate? Can you
    think of any specific instances which make you

feel the way you do? Try to be as concrete as possible.

5. Did you have a happy childhood? Did you live in a happy home? If so, what was it that made it so? If not, what could have changed that would have made the situation better? Do you believe in the statement that you carry your primary family around with you wherever you go?

Chapter Two

An Inner World

Neverland is not a place. It is locked up deep within our minds. It is an imaginary world difficult to find and even harder to get to. You cannot get there by land, or by sea, or by air. You cannot even get there by consciously trying to imagine it. On the contrary, you must be led there by another and allow its delectable shores to come to you.

Mapping the Mind

Neverland dwells in the land of our dreams. It is different for everyone, yet strangely familiar to us all. It is difficult to describe because each person imagines it (and therefore perceives it) in a slightly different fashion.

For Wendy's brother John, it has a lagoon with flamingoes flying over it; for her little brother Michael, however, it has a flamingo with lagoons flying over it. John lives on the sands in an overturned boat; Michael, in a wigwam; Wendy, in a house of leaves. John has no friends; Michael's friends keep him company at night; Wendy has an orphaned pet wolf.

By and large, our individual Neverlands resemble one another in much the same way that physical traits are shared by family members and passed on from one generation to the next. The similarities in our different Neverlands far outweigh their dissimilarities. Perhaps this is so because, deep down inside, we know we all belong to the same human family.

Children know this instinctively. That is why they are forever finding their way to the beaches of these strange lands. They live and play with one foot in the Neverland and one foot in the land of their birth. At times, they break through the veil separating the two worlds and enter it completely. This is exactly what happens to Wendy and her brothers when they fly away with Peter.

To get a glimpse of Neverland, it is necessary to understand the inner workings of a child's mind. Although the human psyche can be mapped out in much the same way as the human anatomy, a child's mind is especially difficult since confusion holds sway there and forces everything to go round and round. The convoluted and zigzag lines of a child's mind reveal the inner island roads of Neverland. Whoever travels them must beware of not losing their way. Otherwise, they may share the shadowy fate of the lost boys and may never make their way back.

The Darling children, however, are far from lost. They have their mother to look after them. Like any good mother, Mrs. Darling tidies up Wendy, John, and Michael's minds each evening as they sleep, rummaging through the disorderly rubble of the day, folding and repacking, making things ready for tomorrow. It is during one such nightly cleaning that she comes across the word "Peter" in John and Michael's minds and especially in Wendy's. It makes her wonder at first, for she knows no one by that name. She then remembers a time in her own childhood when she believed in a boy by that name who lived with the fairies. But that was long, long ago. Now a sensible adult with a husband and children to look after, she very much doubts if any such person ever existed—a fatal mistake if ever there was one.

Looking Deeper

Neverland is the name for the inner world of a child's imagination. Children have a unique capacity for creating the wildest of situations and pretending as though they were real. They are not content with simply imitating those around them. In addition to wanting to be doctors and nurses, policemen and firemen, fathers and mothers, they also invent imaginary worlds which mirror the world in which they live, but which also go far beyond the normal confines of human experience. Neverland is the name for such worlds born in and of a child's mind. Whatever it looks like, it is constantly changing since a child's imagination is always in a state of flux. Change comes easily for children. Their capacity for imagining helps them to process the world around them and sharpens their ability to adapt to the world around them. Few words are as imaginative and exciting as the simple phrase, "Let's pretend." All children say them or, at the very least, wish to say them. Most do so many times each day.

This capacity to live in a world of make-believe is what separates the world of the child from the world of the adult. As we get older, we gradually lose touch with the imaginary powers of our childhood. We do so partly out of necessity and partly out of choice. Few of us choose to remain children (as if we ever could). Most of us cannot wait until we are all grown up. It is only once we have crossed the line from childhood to adulthood (just when that occurs is as different in each person as his or her fingerprint) that we look back with nostalgic regret and realize what we have lost. Coping with that sense of loss is one of the major tasks of our adult life. Those who integrate it with the other dimensions of their personality tap into and often recapture some of the imaginative vigor of their youth (although never completely). Those who do not run the risk of having their hearts run dry and their memories atrophied. How well have you fared in this very difficult task?

Reflection Questions

1. If someone were to map your mind, what would it look like? Would it be any different from the map of your childhood mind? Would you re-

cognize any similarities between the two? Any differences?

2. Do you remember what your childhood Neverland looked like? Think hard. Try to remember its contours, features, and shapes. Has it been a long time since you have tried to remember it? Have you ever shared your childhood imaginings with anyone else?

3. Wendy has a pet wolf in her imaginary world. Have you ever had any imaginary friends? Who or what were they? What were their names? What did you do with them? Do you miss them? How long has it been since you have seen them?

4. Do you miss your childhood? What do you miss most about it? What do you not miss? Do you ever feel as though you have lost touch with your childhood? What do you think could be done to get back in touch with it?

5. Have you ever in your adult life gotten a glimpse into the Neverland of your early life? If not, do you ever wish you could? If so, what happened? How did it occur? Has it changed your life in any way?

Chapter Three

Losing Your Shadow

Neverland is a place of light and shadow. Those who go there encounter their greatest hopes and deepest fears. Children go there to confront the often unwieldy forces of the real world through a steady regimen of make-believe. Neverland promises excitement and adventure to all who walk its shores and penetrate its deep island forests. While there, one never quite knows what to expect. One thing alone is certain. Eventually, one will either find or lose oneself. Only Peter, the perennial exception to the rule, manages to escape this difficult existential choice. Even he, however, loses his shadow for a time.

The Lost Shadow

On one particular night, Nana has the evening off and Mrs. Darling, having put her children to sleep, is quietly sewing at their bedside. After a while she nods off and dreams that Neverland has come too close to her children and that a strange boy has broken through from it.

At the very moment when she dreams that the nursery window has blown open, this strange little boy actually pops into the room. He is accompanied by Tinker Bell, a bright fairy light who darts about the room every which way. Her radiant light wakens Mrs. Darling who, looking at the small boy dressed in skeleton leaves, knows at once that it is Peter Pan. Peter, in turn, looks at Mrs. Darling and, realizing she is a grown-up, gnashes his teeth at her.

At this unexpected welcome, Mrs. Darling lets out a startling scream. Her cry arouses Nana who, having just returned from her evening out, runs through the door, growls, and then springs after Peter. Nana's heroics send the evening intruder springing lightly through the window and out into the starry night. His escape, however, is not complete, since Nana closes the window shut just in the nick of time to catch the boy's shadow in it. Mrs. Dowling takes the shadow from Nana and, not knowing quite what to do with it, finally decides to roll it up and put it away carefully in a drawer.

Peter comes back a week later to find what he has lost. This time, the Darlings are out for the evening, and Nana is tied up in the yard by Mr. Darling for uncovering a childish trick he has played on his children (pretending to take his medicine while pouring it into her bowl instead). Peter sweeps through the room with Tink and looks everywhere for his shadow. At first, he has no luck, but Tink eventually finds it in the drawer where Mrs. Darling left it. Peter is elated at this discovery but saddened when he cannot reattach his shadow to his foot with the bathroom soap. His failure to do so leaves him pouting on the floor on the verge of tears. His crying awakens Wendy, who politely introduces herself to the boy and, seeing his predicament, offers to sew his shadow back on for him at the heel of his foot. This she does (much to Peter's delight), a task which makes Tink jealous, but which also earns for her a trip to a far-off land. Within minutes, Peter has taught Wendy and her brothers to fly and convinced them to come away with him for a visit to the Neverland.

Looking Deeper

Peter brings both shadow and light into Wendy's room. Within minutes of his first visit, he loses his shadow and leaves only with the bright fairy light. Peter's home is Neverland. That is where he feels most at home. That is the place where he has chosen to live and to be. In the real world, Peter not only does not feel at home but somehow becomes unreal. Even when he comes back and finds his shadow with Tinker Bell's help, he is rendered helpless and forced to cry like a baby, stopping only when Wendy befriends him and eases his predicament with some needle and thread. In the real world, everyone has a shadow. Peter loses his shadow because he cannot stand the sight of the adult world as represented by the charming Mrs. Darling. He cannot stand the thought of growing up.

Wendy is just the opposite. She reacts to Peter in much the same way that Mrs. Darling would act toward her. She mothers Peter, attaching his shadow carefully to his foot and even offering to iron it for him. She also acts toward him in a romantic fashion, in much the same way that Mrs. Darling acts toward Mr. Darling. Peter likes the former but does not quite understand the latter. When Wendy offers to kiss him, he agrees and sticks out his hand in eager anticipation. Not wishing to embarrass him, Wendy puts a thimble in his hand and calls it a kiss. Peter reciprocates by placing an acorn button in her hand, a token of friendship which she puts on a chain and wears around her neck. Peter's "kiss" would later save Wendy's life.

Tinker Bell and Wendy, the two principal feminine characters of the story, are the ones who reunite Peter with his shadow: Tinker Bell finds it for him; Wendy attaches it for him. The former is a luminous sprite capable of great heroics but also petty jealousies; the latter is flesh and blood little girl who, at one and the same time, is both fascinated by Peter and sorry for him. That Peter even enters the real world, comes back for his shadow, and allows Wendy to reattach it shows at least a faint desire on his part to acquaint himself with the real world and go through the painful process of growing up. That he dazzles Wendy and her brothers with exciting promises and tall tales of adventure in the Neverland shows that he is not yet ready to grow up (and perhaps never will be). At this point of the story, neither are any of the Darling children.

Reflection Questions

1. Is your life filled with light and shadow? A mixture of the two? How do they relate? Are there any gray areas in your life? If so, what are they? Do you associate any particular images or symbols with the areas of shadow and light in your life? What do they mean to you?

2. Have you ever felt as though you were a stranger to yourself? Have you ever felt out of touch with your darker, weaker side? When are you most apt to feel this way? How have you coped with the shadow side of your personality? Did anyone help you confront this side of your personality?

3. Have the coping mechanisms you have used to deal with the darkness in your life enriched your life or made it worse? Have they enabled you to grow or kept you from growing? Are you happy or unhappy with the progress you have made?

4. Have you ever regretted growing up? Did you ever wish you had remained a child all your life? Was there ever a time in your life when you simply did not want to face the challenges of adult life? What, in your opinion, was the most diffi-

cult part about being a child? About growing up? About being an adult?

5. Are you at peace with yourself? Are you happy with the decisions you have made about your life? Do you have any regrets? Is there anything you would like to change? What kind of person do you see yourself as being ten years from now?

Chapter Four

Coming and Going

"Second to the right, and straight on till morning." Peter's directions to Neverland cannot be followed by anyone other than himself, especially since he always says just anything that comes into his head. He tells Wendy and her brothers that they can fly simply by thinking lovely, wonderful thoughts, when in reality no one can fly without touching fairy dust. He loves to trifle with his new friends—and to tell tall tales. His stories of mermaids, pirates, and Indians so excite Wendy, John, and Michael that they accept Peter's invitation and are up and flying before they know it. It takes them a while to feel comfortable with their newfound skill but, before long, they are zooming through the air and following Peter's lead on the way to Neverland.

Looking for Stories

Peter wants Wendy to come with him so that she can tell stories to him and the other lost boys of Neverland, orphaned children who fell out of their perambulators soon after birth. He also wants her to take care of them: cook for them and darn their clothing the way any mother would. "One girl is more use than twenty boys," Peter tells her.

Actually, it is Wendy who first puts the idea of her going to Neverland into Peter's head. "Oh, the stories I could tell to the boys!" Although she eagerly wishes to accompany him back to Neverland, she worries about leaving home and the pain her parents would go through. Peter, however, is relentless. As soon as the idea pops into his mind, he takes possession of it and naturally thinks it is his own. He lures Wendy with all sorts of promises like learning to fly, meeting mermaids, keeping house—to name but a few. It is his overtures toward her motherly instincts that probably wins her over. How can she resist his invitation of allowing her to tuck him and the other lost boys in at night?

Convincing John and Michael is the easy part. Peter is indifferent to teaching them how to fly, but he knows that Wendy is not about to leave her little brothers behind on what is likely to be the adventure of her life—and theirs! Before they know it, they are out the window and circling church spires and other tall buildings. On their way to Neverland, Peter teaches them how to swoop up and down at different speeds. He saves them from death when they fall asleep and start plummeting toward earth. He also teaches them how to grab food from the mouths of birds and to engage in a seemingly endless game of chase.

Looking Deeper

Peter leaves Neverland and finds his way to the window of Wendy's bedroom because he is enamored of the stories Mrs. Darling tells her children just before they go to sleep. There is something about a story that brings movement and excitement to the life of a child. Night after night, he listens by the window and then returns to Neverland to tell the other boys what has happened. For the past few nights, Mrs. Darling has been narrating the story of Cinderella. He wonders how it will end and does not have a clue. When Wendy tells him, he gets excited and cannot wait to leave for Neverland to inform his friends. He is their captain, you see.

Everyone loves a good story, and Peter Pan is no exception. Listening to the unfolding of a good story puts one in touch with some of the deepest rhythms of life. Stories bring a sense of drama to life. They offer meaning, excitement, and closure. They are vehicles of expression. They also teach. A good story captivates the listener and transports him or her to another world. In doing so, it enables one to view one's own world in a different light. Stories also provide a sense of comfort and security. A good bedtime story is the perfect way for a mother to ease her child from the world of consciousness to the unconscious world of sleep. Stories are also a good way of tucking a small child in at night. They ready them for their dreams and ease their fears about what the night might bring them. Peter and the lost boys long for someone to tell them stories. When he discovers the wealth of stories in Wendy's repertoire, he does everything in his power to convince her to leave everything behind and enter the magical world of Neverland.

Wendy, of course has mixed feelings about leaving the safe and familiar surroundings of her family home and entering a world so strange and foreign as Neverland. She wants to go, but also does not want to go. She is excited by all that Peter lays before her, but also very scared. She wants to make the journey but also wishes to stay behind. In the end, it is her desire to grow up, her deeply ingrained wish to be a mother to the lost boys, that moves her to take the risk.

Wendy's trip to Neverland is a necessary step on her long journey through childhood into adolescence and then adulthood. Peter and the lost boys give her the opportunity to express herself in ways that she never would have been able to do if she had stayed behind in the secure and predictable ways of everyday life. By entering the magical shores of Neverland, she assumes roles she had previously only dreamed of. From the very moment she leaves the safety of the Darling nursery, she assumes the role of a responsible and caring mother.

Reflection Questions

1. What stories did you like to listen to when you were a child? Did you have any favorites? Was there someone in particular whom you pre-

ferred to tell them? Your mother? Your father? An aunt or uncle? An older brother or sister? Was a special time in the day set aside for stories? After lunch? Before nap time? Before going to bed?

2. Did you ever try to lure someone into trying to doing something for you? What tactics did you use? What did you promise him or her? Did you do everything at your disposal to get your way? Did it work? Were you happy you did it? Was it worth it?

3. What did you most like to pretend to be when you were a little child? Was it a particular person? A particular occupation? A combination of both? Did your choice change through the years? Did your choice affect your later life decisions in any way? If so in what ways?

4. What is your earliest memory of having mixed feelings about something? Can you think of anything in your life that you wanted and did not want at the same time? Have you ever experienced simultaneously both a like and a dislike for the same person? If so, what brought such feelings on? How did you deal with these feelings?

5. Do you remember ever trying to enter com-
    pletely into a world of make-believe? Did you
    find it difficult? How long could you sustain it?
    Did it benefit you in any way? Did it have any
    liabilities? Were you always happy to leave your
    world of make-believe? Were you happy to
    make your way home?

Chapter Five

Round and Round

After seemingly endless days of travel, Peter and his friends see a million golden arrows pointing out the island of Neverland off in the distance. As they approach it, they see the Mysterious River and are able to recognize its various features from their memory of it in their dreams. The closer they get, the more Neverland is enveloped in darkness. The children are used to dreaming about Neverland in the safety of their beds with Nana watching over them and with the night-lights on. If Neverland was make-believe in those days, it now seems very real to them. They feel a throb of excitement, the fear of the unknown, the risk of high adventure.

A Circular Chase

As they get even closer, they look down over the island and see Neverland waking to life and get a bird's eye view of the circular chase that defines much of the daily life on the magic island: "The lost boys were out looking for Peter, the pirates were out looking for the lost boys, the redskins were out looking for the pirates, and the beasts were out looking for the redskins. They were going round and round the island, but they did not meet because all were going at the same rate."

Also on the island is a crocodile in constant search for Hook, the feared captain of a motley pirate crew. This crocodile received a taste of Hook's flesh a long time ago when Peter severed the captain's arm in a heated fight and tossed it casually into its mouth (an offense for which Hook has never forgiven Peter). The crocodile liked the taste of Hook so much that it searches for him day and night from sea to sea and from land to land. Hook is deathly afraid of it. He shudders in fear every time he hears the approach of the strong ticking sound emanating from its belly, the fortuitous result of a clock it had somehow managed to swallow in its ravenous search for food.

As they approach the island, Tinker Bell, who, like any fairy, is so small that she only has room for one feeling at a time and who has been hidden in John's hat to hide her fairy light, vents her jealousy of Wendy in a terrible way. The group is separated for a while after a thunderous crash from Long Tom, the pirates' deadly canon. In the confusion, Tink gets Wendy's attention and leads her to within eyesight of the lost boys. When they see Wendy, they mistake her for a bird and Tink yells out to them "Peter wants you to shoot the Wendy!" Tootles, the most unfortunate but also the humblest of the lot follows Tink's words. All of the lost boys rejoice at the kill (especially Tootles), and all are filled with remorse when they realize that he did not kill a bird but a lady. Fortunately, Wendy is wearing around her neck the acorn button given her by Peter at their first meeting. This keepsake blocks Tootles arrow and prevents serious injury.

Looking Deeper

Getting to Neverland is itself an adventure of a lifetime. Endless days of flight pass in an instant, but an instant lasts an eternity. Wendy and her brothers follow Peter not through time and space, but through the darkened corridors of the mind. Thinking is out; imagination, in. When Peter and his companions finally see the island's magic shores off in the distance, they sense the ominous nature of the journey they are really about to undertake. For Peter, it is a homecoming; for Wendy and her brothers, it is a foreign yet strangely familiar place. For all of them, danger lurks everywhere, and they encounter it sooner than they may have expected.

The inhabitants of the island are involved in an endless chase that goes on at the same pace and without intermission. There is a strong theatrical quality to it, one that gives the reader the sense that all the participants are, at one and the same time, both pretending yet deathly serious. This strange juxtaposition of conflicting premises provides the pretext for the extended game of life and death being played on the magic island. How so? One gets the strong sense that, once the lost boys find Peter, the chase will instantaneously reverse itself in the opposite direction. Indeed, the only chase that remains constant throughout the story is the crocodile's unrelenting hunt for Captain Hook. Its ceaseless ticking is a harsh intrusion of reality into this otherwise thoroughly insulated world of make-believe. Time marches on and will one day catch up with its prey. Hook is doomed at the very outset. The reader knows instinctively that it is only a matter of time before the crocodile enjoys once again the tasty morsels of the pirate's flesh.

Strong psychological forces are also vying with each other on this imaginary island. Wendy has barely arrived when a jealousy-driven Tinker Bell hatches a deadly plot. Tink represents that side of the feminine that feels easily threatened and will go to great lengths to get what it wants. She represents the immature side of any person who becomes so immersed in a single emotion that he or she is unable to act in a mature, even-handed manner. Tinker Bell hates Wendy and acts upon it; Wendy almost dies on account of her. Tinker Bell presents a clear and constant danger to Wendy both from without and from within. If the contours of Neverland represent the author's attempt to map a child's mind, the reader must recognize the possibility that Wendy's growth from a child to an adult will involve being able to deal with more than one emotion at a time and to integrate the wide range of feelings possible with her heart and mind.

Reflection Questions

1. Have you ever tried to map out the various tensions and antagonisms of the world around you? Who is chasing who? Where do you fit into the picture? Do you ever feel as though everyone is going round and round in an endless chase?

2. Does your life ever feel like an ongoing drama? If so, who are the major characters in it? How would you describe them? Which ones have had the greatest influence on you? The least? If you could, how would you change in this ongoing drama known as your life? How would you like it to end?

3. Do you ever feel chased by time? What is your reaction to it? Do you run from it? Ignore it? Confront it? Are you afraid of the onward march of time? If so, do you understand why you feel the way you do? Can you think of any constructive ways of coping with such fears?

4. Have you ever decided to do something only to find out later that the result did much more harm than good? What toll did this decision take on your self-confidence and sense of well-

being? Did it make you more careful with your decisions? More timid? Afraid? Humble?

5. What psychological forces are at work in your life right now? Which are stronger: the constructive ones such as love and friendship, or the destructive ones such as jealousy and hatred? If the latter, do you know how to process them? Work through them? Do you believe that love has a healing effect on the soul?

Chapter Six

Building and Playing House

Peter arrives on the scene after Tootles shoots Wendy down but before they discover that she is still alive. He tells the lost boys that he has brought a mother to them at long last and asks if they have seen her flying by. Tootles comes forth and confesses his crime to Peter who, in turn, curses his cowardly hand and raises an arrow to kill him. All during this time, however, Wendy is slowly waking from unconsciousness. She raises her arm and magically stays Peter's hand. When they realize that Wendy is still with them, they rejoice in their new-found mother and resolve not to bring her down to their underground home (her present state of health is too delicate for such a move), but to build a house around her above ground.

The Little House

Peter and the lost boys set about building a little house right where Wendy is lying. They gut their underground house and bring up the best they have. They gather bedding for her and firewood. They bring up a chair and table for her. At one point, Wendy's brothers, John and Michael, come upon the scene, and they too are conscripted to work on the project and, before long, find themselves hacking and hewing and carrying.

When they have all the interior furnishings, they start building the little house around it. "Ay," said Slightly, "that's how a house is built; it all comes back to me." Peter, it seems, thought of everything—even calling for a doctor to examine Wendy. At this command, Slightly disappears for a spell and returns with John's hat on his head and acting very dignified. He examines Wendy, places a glass thing in her mouth, and proclaims Wendy cured. Everyone seems to be involved in this extended game of make-believe. The main difference between Peter and the other boys seems to be that they know they are just pretending, whereas for Peter making-believe is real. He wraps the lost boys on the knuckles whenever they stop playing the game.

Before long, Peter and the lost boys are putting the finishing touches on the house. Tootles uses the heel of his shoe as a door knocker. Peter takes the bottom out of John's hat and places it on the roof to serve as a chimney. When all is complete, they knock on the door and Wendy comes out. She admires her new house and promises to be their mother. At that, she marches them straightaway inside, where she tucks them in bed and finishes the story of Cinderella for them before they fall fast asleep.

Peter stands guard over the house during the night to protect Wendy, her brothers, and the lost boys from the danger of a surprise attack by pirates or Indians. The next day, he has Wendy, John, and Michael fitted for hollow trees, the personalized chutes that gave them easy access to the underground house. Once this is done, Wendy and her brothers join Peter and the lost boys in their underground home, which consists of one large room with stout mushrooms that are used as stools and a large Never tree growing in the middle. This tree is cut down to size at various times during the day either to provide more space for play or to serve as a makeshift table.

Wendy is kept very busy taking care of her boys in their underground home. She cooks for them, mends their clothes, watches out for them, scolds them and, most of all, tells them stories. It is hard to say how long this goes on, for time moves at a very different pace in Neverland. For Wendy and her brothers, life in Neverland passes happily by, moving from one adventurous day to the next (life with Peter and the lost boys was never boring). Although she does not worry about her parents, since she knows that they will always leave the window open for her to fly back, she does worry that her brothers are beginning to forget them. To correct this, she begins questioning them about their parents and the rest of the Darling household, an exercise which she carries out regularly and which the other lost boys like to share in.

Looking Deeper

Very clear roles are defined in this massive game of make-believe. Peter and the lost boys take good care of Wendy. They shelter her, protect her, and nurse her back to health until she is able to join them in their underground home. As the lost boy's beloved captain, Peter even assumes a fatherly role for a while—one that he does not sustain for very long. Wendy, in turn, takes good care of them. She mothers them to their hearts' content by cooking for them, sewing for them, disciplining them, and telling them stories. She sustains the role longer than any of them, but never manages to forget her roots.

The move from the little house on the surface to the underground home has special significance, for it symbolizes a move from the conscious to the unconscious. This place is where Peter and the lost boys make their home. They embark each day on their adventures on the surface of Neverland, but they sleep and are nurtured below ground. They dream in this place and set out from it each day in search of high adventure. This underground home is very important for each one of them, so much so that each of the lost boys can get there only through a hollow tree trunk specially fitted to his size. What is more, with Wendy to care for them, their deepest dream has finally come true. They have a mother to care for them, and they are all exceedingly happy.

In assuming the motherly role in the underground home, Wendy performs much the same task that her mother, Mrs. Darling, did for her children as they slept. Keeping house here is Wendy's way of tidying up her children's minds. She does so in a way that brings comfort, order, and security to the lives of Peter and the lost boys, but which also gives free rein to the imagination. Wendy does such a good job that she is beginning to worry about her brothers, John and Michael. They are in danger of losing touch with their real home and of becoming one of the lost boys. To prevent this from happening, she goads their memories of what life was like in their real home. The implication is important: just as imagination is what ties a child's mind to Neverland, memory is what ties it into the real world. Both are nurtured in a healthy child and interact in a variety of ways.

Reflection Questions

1. When you were child, did you prefer building houses or playing house? Which roles were you apt to play in them? Were they active or passive? Major or minor? Were you happy with the roles

you played or did you always want to play someone else?

2. Do you remember any of the dreams that you
   had as a child? Did they make you happy or sad?
   Did they frighten you? Have you ever seen a
   connection between your semi-conscious dream
   life and your ability to pretend?

3. When you were a child, did you ever have a
   difficult time distinguishing between the real
   world and the world of make-believe? How did
   these two worlds interact for you? Did they ever
   touch? Become fused? Did one ever seem to
   permeate the other? What role did memory play
   in helping you draw the distinction?

4. Are your parents still alive? Did they tidy up
   your mind when you were young? Can you
   picture them in a scene from your childhood?
   What are they saying to you? Is there anything
   you would like to say to them? Do you think
   there are any experiences which you may have
   unconsciously blocked from your memory? Do
   you have any idea what they may be?

5. What is your underground home like? Is it any
   different from when you were a child? How is it
   furnished? Who lives there with you? How often

do you go there? Who else is allowed in? What
do you do there? Who takes care of you?

Chapter Seven

The Mermaids' Lagoon

Peter and the lost boys have so many adventures that the narrator admits it would take a book the size of the English-Latin, Latin-English Dictionary to contain them all. Since one adventure is as good as the next, he has a difficult time selecting one for his readers. A flip of the coin selects the adventure of the Mermaids' Lagoon.

Marooner's Rock

The children of Neverland love to spend long summer days swimming and floating in this colorful pool of water. There, mermaids sing and play, hitting bubbles with their tails and playing other such games. They generally keep to themselves and, except for Peter, are not on friendly terms with children.

One day, Wendy and the boys are on Marooner's Rock, a larger boulder (about the size of a large bed) in the middle of the lagoon that becomes submerged each night with the rising tide. Evil captains have been known to tie sailors up and leave them there to drown in the rising water. In the early afternoon, however, it is generally a safe and frequent gathering place for those playing in the lagoon.

After lunch, Wendy beds the children down on the rock for their afternoon nap and busies herself with some sewing. Unaccustomed to the dangers of the lagoon, she does not sense any evil lurking near them. Peter, however, intuits something deep in his sleep and, rising up instinctively, cries out that there are pirates in the area. Everyone wakes up, dives into the water, and keeps their senses attuned to the trouble that awaits them.

Within a few moments, they see Starkey and Smee, two of Hook's henchmen rowing toward the rock with Tiger Lily, the Indian princess of the Piccaninny tribe. She has been captured by Hook and his men and, bound hand and foot, is about to be left on the rock to die with the rising tide. Feeling she is unevenly matched (2 against 1), Peter saves Tiger Lily by imitating Hook's voice and ordering the two pirates to cut her loose and let her go.

Just after they do this, the real Hook approaches, who tells his men that Peter and the lost boys have found a mother called "Wendy." As they scheme of capturing Wendy so that she can be their mother, he learns of Tiger Lily's escape and senses that something has gone afoul. At this point, Peter imitates Hook's voice a second time. He accuses Hook of being an impostor and calls him a codfish. They banter back and forth until Peter reveals his true identity.

At that moment, all hell breaks loose. Peter and the lost boys engage Hook and his henchmen in a heated battle. Peter battles Hook on the rock and, startled by the evil captain's lack of fair play (he bites the boy after receiving a courtesy), is badly wounded in his side. Hook cannot finish Peter off, however, because he hears the ticking of the crocodile and strikes off madly for his ship, the Jolly Roger, with his two henchmen not far behind.

In all the confusion, the lost boys return to shore because they think Peter and Wendy have gone on ahead of them. Wendy, in reality, has made her way to the rock and discovers Peter and his wounds. The two are now alone and in a terrible predicament. Evening is approaching and the waters are beginning to rise. Peter can neither fly nor swim because of his wounds. No one can hear their cries for help. Wendy is too tired to swim ashore unaided.

A kite made by Michael some days before and which somehow tore from his hands flies by mysteriously. Peter grabs it and, since it is sturdy enough for one passenger, insists that Wendy go back with it to shore. Wendy protests, but Peter will hear none of it. He sends her to safety and awaits his approaching death. "To die will be an awfully big adventure," he says.

Looking Deeper

Even a magic island like Neverland needs a place for rest and relaxation. The Mermaids' Lagoon provides just that for Wendy and the boys. They play in the water to their hearts content, the way children are apt to spend their long summer days at the beach. Their fun and excitement, however, pale in comparison to the mermaids, who keep their distance playing with bubbles made of rainbow water, hitting them back and forth with their tails. The mermaids represent a child's endless fascination with water. They are a feminine principle representing a child's unconscious desire for a return to the womb, a desire which, at one and the same time both lures them closer and keeps them further away.

Marooner's Rock, by way of contrast, symbolizes danger in the midst of such tranquility. A rising phallic symbol surrounded by water, it is a masculine principle which pits itself against the forces of the rising tide, a natural phenomenon reminding us of the cycles of life. For those numbered among the living, it also stands for the steady approach of death, which no one can escape or fend off—not even in Neverland. It is no accident that Peter and Hook square off with one another on the Marooner's Rock since they represent the two extreme dangers every little boy (and girl) faces in life: the child who consciously refuses to grow up, and the person who grows up at the expense of losing all contact with his or her childhood memories. It bears noting that both types live in Neverland and not the real world. One is lost in time; the other is forever running away from it. Each thrives on fantasy rather than on life experience—and each rarely learns from his mistakes.

All the other events of the adventure of the Mermaids' Lagoon must be seen against the backdrop of these underlying psychic tensions. Wendy's motherly care for the boys on Marooner's Rock, Tiger Lily's capture and escape, Peter's imitation of Hook, the fight with the pirates, the wound in Peter's side, the timely appearance of the crocodile, Wendy's escape on a kite, Peter's resolve to face the adventure of death are all responses by one or more of the characters to the tensions outlined above. When seen in this light, the adventure of the Mermaids' Lagoon encapsulates all of the book's major themes and presents the reader with a scaled-down version of the larger work.

Reflection Questions

1. Where is the Mermaids' Lagoon in your life? Did you go there often as a child? Where do you go now when you want to be totally relaxed? What do you do? Who is with you? What kind of environment helps you to lay back, play, and simply be yourself?

2. Do you think you have ever had any unconscious or conscious desires to return to the

womb? If so, what are those desires like? Can you describe them? How do they make you feel? Act? Do you enjoy them? Do you think they are normal? Are you happy you have them? Are you shamed of them in any way?

3. What is your reaction to being treated unfairly? Does it stun you? Incapacitate you for a while? Do you expect it? Does it make you angry? Does it make you want to do the same to others? Or does it strengthen your resolve to treat others fairly and with respect?

4. Is there a part of you that has refused to grow up? Is there a part of you that has lost touch with your childhood? Which of these parts is stronger? Do you struggle with them? Are they in any way related?

5. Do you think about dying much? At all? Does the thought of dying scare you? Does it affect in any way your understanding of life? Does it affect the way you live? Have you ever thought of death as an awfully big adventure?

Chapter Eight

The Never Bird

The adventure in the Mermaid's Lagoon is actually a double adventure, for it also includes the story of the Never bird and its selfless efforts to save Peter from certain death. When he first comes to Marooner's Rock, Hook notices the Never bird off to the distance, sitting on its nest which had fallen from a tree and was floating in the lagoon. Little does he know that the bird's motherly instinct would also be directed toward Peter.

The Never Nest

Peter is all alone on Marooner's Rock, bleeding from his wounds and watching the gradual rise of the waters around him. The rock is slowly disappearing; the water of the lagoon is lapping at his feet and, before long, will swallow him up completely. As he awaits his fate, Peter espies something floating off in the distance. At first, he thinks it is a piece of paper, perhaps part of the kite which brought Wendy to safety. As the tide brings it closer, he notices that it is the Never bird sitting on her nest and working its wings on the water to move near him. It has come to save him.

Peter had been nice to the bird in the past but, as little boys are wont to do at times, had also been a little nasty to her. Despite those boyish taunts, the Never bird was coming closer to Peter with the intention of giving him her nest as a life raft. She was doing so even though her nest had eggs in it, and she was risking the future of her own offspring. The only credible explanation of her action is that her motherly heart melted when she saw such a young boy like Peter in mortal distress.

The Never bird is exhausted when it finally gets within earshot of Peter. A comical exchange follows when neither can understand what the other is saying. Eventually, the Never bird makes her intentions known when she gives her nest one final push toward the rock, flies into the air, and abandons her eggs. Peter notices that there are two eggs in the nest. He takes them out and wonders what he can do with them. From up above, the Never bird covers her eyes with her feathers, for she cannot bear to witness their fate.

Just then, Peter gets a wonderful idea. He notices a stave in the rock upon which Starkey had hung his deep, broad-rimmed, waterproof tarpaulin hat. He takes down the hat, places it in the water and, seeing that it floats beautifully, gently lays the eggs down in it. Elated at what Peter has done, the Never bird swoops down and nestles herself in place on the hat. Peter then sets up a makeshift mast in the nest with the stave, uses his shirt as a sail, and makes his way to safety.

Wendy and the lost boys are overwhelmed at Peter's return. They pass the hours recounting their adventures one after another. It is only when Wendy realizes the lateness of the hour that she stays their enthusiasm and sends them off to bed. It bears noting that Starkey's hat is a huge success as a nest and that, from that time on, all Never birds decide to build their nests with a broad rim for their chicks to perch on.

Looking Deeper

The Never bird acts to save Peter even when it is against her own interests. To do so, she must act against her natural motherly instincts to nurture and protect her young. She seems to be in touch with a deeper motherly instinct, one that reaches out to protect the vulnerable and motherless. She acts in this way even though she knows full well that Peter has not always treated her with kindness. She is able to overlook Peter's shortcomings and put herself in the place of the mother who is not there to help him and whom he has long forgotten. The Never bird's actions are self-sacrificing and heroic. Her actions seem to surprise Peter and perhaps even herself.

Peter and the Never bird experience a failure to communicate. Each is speaking a different language, and each makes different sense out of the sounds they hear. This failure to understand each other on the verbal level, however, is overcome through motion, gesture, and overall good intentions. Difficult as communication with another may be, such good intentions seldom go unnoticed. For Peter, the Never bird's actions speak louder than the sounds she is making—and vice versa. In the end, both Peter and the Never bird use their actions to make their good intentions known and help each other out in the process.

Creative ideas also enter into the picture. The Never bird is in a difficult situation to begin with. Her nest has fallen into the water, and she has gone with it to protect her young. When she sees Peter in his predicament, the unusual idea comes to her of sending her nest over to him as a life raft. Implementing this idea, however, involves strenuous activity (she must use her wings to draw the nest over to Peter) and great personal cost (she jeopardizes the safety of her unhatched chicks). Peter also finds himself in a difficult situation. When the Never nest has finally reached him, he suddenly gets the idea of using Starkey's hat as a floatation device. Too small for him, it is just right for the eggs. As the waters continue to rise upon Marooner's Rock, he develops his plan and implements it quickly. Before long, both he and the Never eggs are off the rock and out of danger's way. Within a short while, an act of self-sacrifice has turned a life-threatening situation completely around. Even to this day, the tale of the Never bird is recounted with great admiration and respect.

Reflection Questions

1. Do you consider yourself in touch with your deepest instincts? If so, what are they? How would you describe them? Are they constructive or destructive? One or many? Conflicting or harmonious? Have you ever acted on them?

2. Have you ever found yourself in a situation where it was difficult for you to communicate with another person? How difficult was it? What did you do to get through the situation? Did you learn anything about yourself as a result?

3. How do creative ideas come to you? Out of nowhere? When you are in touch with your deepest instincts? With your heart? When you contemplate the world around you? How do you implement them? Are they generally worthwhile?

4. Have you ever benefited from another's self-sacrificing action toward you? How did you react? Did you expect it? Did you think you

deserved it? Did you do anything to elicit such generosity?

5. Have you ever helped another through your self-sacrificing efforts? If so, what was the experience like? Did you risk a great deal? How did it make you feel? How did it make the other person feel? Why did you do it? Would you do it again?

Chapter Nine

The Happy Home

After the dual adventure of the Mermaids' Lagoon and the Never bird, Peter, Wendy, and the boys return home and begin what must be described as a brief but extremely happy time together in their home under the ground. This is a moment in their lives when everything in their world fits exactly in place. Every role is assigned, and each child plays it well. They feel safe, protected, and free. As a result, they are able to find adventure and excitement in the simplest of home activities. They enjoy themselves in this way until that disastrous evening now known to them as the Night of Nights.

Life Underground

Peter's rescue of Tiger Lily endears him to the entire Piccaninny tribe. They call him the Great White Father and promise to protect his family from the pirates. They do so by positioning themselves above the underground home and keeping careful watch for them all during the night. This extra protection allows Peter, Wendy, and the boys to sit back and enjoy the simple pleasures of family life. Wendy continues her role as a loving and caring mother. The boys frolic and play and, of course, complain (as boys are wont to do at that age). Peter, however, assumes more of a fatherly role. He makes decisions, settles disputes, and always has his family's best interests at heart. "Father knows best," Wendy likes to tell her children.

On one particular evening (the one which would turn out to be the last for this happy family), Peter is out gathering nuts and looking for the crocodile so he can find the correct time for Wendy. Wendy and the boys are down below for their evening meal, a make-believe tea. The boys are enjoying themselves but complaining as usual. Slightly complains about Nibs. John wants to occupy Peter's empty chair. Tootles wants to sit in John's basket—and so on. Their complaining is of the usual sort, however, and rises from their deep satisfaction with family life. Around the table, one sees nothing but smiles and contented faces.

When Wendy and the children hear Peter's footsteps above ground, they rush to the door to meet him. As soon as he emerges from his tree, he distributes the nuts and gives Wendy the correct time. The boys then all plead with Peter and Wendy to dance for them. It is Saturday night, after all, and they deserve some entertainment. Peter and Wendy hesitate at first (it isn't *really* Saturday night), but soon comply with their children's wishes. After all, no one but their children will see them.

Wendy puts her hand on Peter's shoulder, and he starts to feel uncomfortable. He begins to blink, as if he is not sure if he is awake or asleep. Not sure of what is real and make-believe, he asks Wendy if he truly is the children's father. She says they are his if he wishes it. She then senses Peter's unease and asks him what his exact feelings are toward her. He tells her that he feels like her devoted son. Expecting another reply, Wendy stops trying to dance with Peter and goes to sit at the other end of the room. She now understands why Tinker Bell is so jealous of her. Both are romantically attracted to Peter and vying for his attention. Peter, however, is hardly aware of their feelings toward him and does not know how to respond. These romantic tensions surface, but never get resolved. Within moments, the rapid pace of their make-believe family life smooths over this intense emotional impasse as Wendy readies her children for bed, tucks them in, and tells them a story.

Looking Deeper

This episode marks the beginning of the end of Wendy's stay in Neverland. In their underground home, Peter, Wendy, and the boys establish a make-believe family with Peter as the father, Wendy as the mother, and the boys as the children. They are enjoying themselves immensely, so much so that the line between make-believe and the real world gets harder and harder for them to distinguish—especially for Peter.

Peter acts the role of father well, although he receives hints from John (one of his supposed children) about just what a father is expected to do. The respect he has gained from the Piccaninny tribe as the Great White Father adds to his sense of authority. Peter has proved himself to be a protector and provider for his family. He also seems to do a good job at maintaining a fatherly relationship with the lost boys. When it comes to romance, however, he is hopelessly uncomfortable and ill-at-ease. He is at that age when he feels no romantic attraction to girls. His lack of awareness infuriates Tinker Bell, who is passionately in love with him, and saddens Wendy. Peter wants to be a devoted son to Wendy. She, however, wants much more from him—and will never receive it.

All of this takes place underground, a symbolic way of pointing out the inner, unconscious reaches of a child's mind. Growing up means allowing these various emotional tensions of one's emerging relationships to come to the surface of one's consciousness so that they can be reflected upon, confronted, and acted upon in mature, constructive ways. These emotions have barely come into Peter's consciousness when personal resistance and external circumstances force them to recede back into the unchartered waters of his mind. This moment in the underground home with Wendy and the boys is the closest Peter will ever get to becoming capable of sustaining real family relationships. The unexpected (and dangerous) twist of events that follow push Peter back into his comfortable role of captain of the lost boys, a role which allows him to disdain the company of adults and the relationships that go along with them. Wendy, on the other hand, has allowed a vast array of emotions to emerge within her consciousness and is willing to allow them to grow and develop. Unlike Peter, she refuses to forget her family of origins and maintains a healthy distinction between reality and the world of make-believe.

Reflection Questions.

1. Can you remember a time in your life when everything seemed to fit together? If so, what made it so nice? Who was responsible for it? What part did you play in making it so? If not, what would it mean for you today to have a life where everything fits together?

2. When you were a child, did you ever find yourself pretending to be in love with another? If so, did you find it easy or difficult? Was it easier than playing house? Did you pretend by yourself or with others? Do you think it helped you to process such feelings when they came?

3. Do you complain a lot? Do you complain in different ways? Are there different degrees of

your complaining? Do you believe that it is possible to complain and to be content at the same time? In your opinion, is this a mature or a childish way of acting? Why?

4. Does pretending help or hinder a child's ability to deal with his or her relationships in the real world? Does it depend on what he or she is pretending? Does the use of stock stereotypes have any affect? Does the act of pretending itself have something to contribute or detract from a child's well-being?

5. How old were you when you started to have romantic feelings for another? Did it take a long time for these feelings to emerge? How did you deal with them? Did you have anyone to talk these feelings over with?

Chapter Ten

Wendy's Story

Each night Wendy is accustomed to telling her children a bedtime story. On this particular night, she relates the story of the Darling household. Peter hates this story because it further reminds Wendy, her brothers, and now the lost boys of life beyond the make-believe world of Neverland. When he challenges Wendy's claim that all mothers keep their windows open for their children to return home, he unknowingly lets loose the very psychological and emotional forces that will hasten the Darling children's return to their parents' home.

Once Upon a Time

Wendy tells the children of what life was like before she and her brothers flew off with Peter to Neverland. She uses the third person and relates it almost as if it were a fairy-tale. She tells them of a gentleman named Mr. Darling, of his wife, Mrs.

Darling, of their three children, and of Nana, their faithful Newfoundland dog who serves as their nurse. She tells them of the events leading up to Peter's visit to the nursery and of their decision to fly away with him to Neverland.

The children are fascinated by the story. The lost boys question Wendy at every turn and are especially pleased to discover that they, too, are part of the story. One special twist to her telling of the story, the part that Peter does not like, is when she asks her eager listeners to consider the feelings of the unhappy parents who miss their children terribly and who are anxiously awaiting their return. Asked if they ever *do* return, Wendy takes an imaginative peep into the future and describes what she, John, and Michael will look like in their adult years. Wendy then extols the greatness of a mother's love saying that the heroine always knew that her mother would leave the window open for them to return. The children stayed away for years, she claims, but returned through the window and had a happy reunion with their parents that words could not describe.

At this point, Peter objects saying that he once thought the way Wendy does but that when he returned to his bedroom window after staying away for many, many moons, he found that his mother had forgotten all about him and that another boy was sleeping in his bed. (The narrator here interjects that it is not certain whether this was true or not, but that Peter certainly *thought* it was true.)

Peter's remarks so scare the children that John and Michael want to go home right away, and even Wendy herself begins to wonder if her mother is only in half mourning by this time. She promptly decides that she and her brothers will return home at once and asks Peter to make the necessary arrangements. Peter agrees and steps outside to do so. When he returns, he will hear nothing of the lost boys' plan to keep Wendy in Neverland as their mother against her will by taking her prisoner. Wendy then gets the idea that *all* the boys could come home with her and live in the Darling household. At that, the lost boys are simply elated—all, that is, except Peter, who refuses to go.

Looking Deeper

Wendy's story serves many purposes. It helps her and her brothers to keep the memory of their parents alive in their hearts. It extols the virtues of a mother's love for her children and leaves open the possibility of an eventual return from Neverland. It also stirs the imagination of the lost boys and makes them yearn for what, in Neverland, they can only experience by pretending. Peter dislikes the story because it loosens Neverland's hold over his companions and signals their desire to return home and continue the process of growing up. For Peter, it is one thing pretending to be an adult. Actually becoming one, however, is an entirely different story.

Nostalgia for home first moves Wendy to tell her story. She has already made great efforts to ensure that John and Michael do not forget their family origins. Using their real lives as a bedtime story reinforces their memories of their parents even more and has the added advantage of keeping the desire for their real home alive in their hearts. In telling this story, Wendy does more than just relate facts and figures. She uses the story not simply to describe the Darling household, but also to help her brothers put themselves in their parents' place. Wendy does this very well; her brothers, much less; the lost boys, hardly; Peter, not at all.

In Neverland, Wendy's story comes across almost as a fairy-tale where there is a happy ending and everything is as it should be. Interestingly enough, it is Peter who points out some of the weaknesses of Wendy's story, by pointing out both the limits of a mother's love and also her capacity to forget. Such harsh realities make him prefer the world of make-believe to the world of the Darling household. Peter's desire to deflate the impact of Wendy's story, however, actually has a reverse effect on them. Rather than lowering their regard for the real world, it makes them realize that their window for reentry into it may soon be closing for them. Worried about what might happen, Wendy decides to return home as soon as possible. Within moments, life in the happy underground home has come to a halt. Everyone but Peter packs up and goes to the surface where the Indians are waiting to guide them through the wood and where, from there, Tinker Bell will lead them across the sea.

Reflection Questions

1. When you were a child, did you ever hear stories about your family? Your forebearers? Are there

any stories about them that you particularly liked or disliked? Do you yourself ever tell any of these stories now? Which ones? Why do you tell them?

2. Do you tell sad or happy stories about your childhood? Perhaps both? Are these stories accurate representations of what your life was really like back then? What do you tend to leave out of the stories? What do you tend to emphasize?

3. What stories do you like to tell about yourself? What stories would you like others to tell about you? Why those stories and not others? How do you tell them or would want them told? What values and emotions would you want them to evoke through them?

4. Has a story you told ever backfired on you? Did it ever convey a sentiment different from the one you originally wanted to evoke? How did it affect other people's lives? Were you able to correct it? Did the story end up taking on a life of its own?

5. What stories do you like to tell about your parents? Did they love you as a child? How did they show it? Did you ever feel as though they

had forgotten about you or had shut you out of their emotional lives? Have you been able to forgive your parents for the harm they may have done to you as a child? Are you able to tell them that you love them?

Chapter Eleven

Carried Off

Just as Wendy and the boys are about to leave their underground home, complete pandemonium breaks out above. The pirates have taken the Indians totally by surprise by positioning themselves on higher ground and attacking first. The Piccaninnies fight bravely but are no match for Hook's clever tactic. Many of the bravest Indians die in the ensuing battle. Eventually, the pirates rout their savage foes and force them to give ground.

Taken Prisoner

Peter, Wendy, and the rest of the children listen to the fierce battle being waged above them. When the fighting is over, a long silence descends over the battlefield and makes its way into their underground home. Uncertain of the victors, they await some kind of a sign. They then hear the sound of a tom-tom above them and recognize it as the traditional signal of an Indian victory. Eager to be on their way, Wendy and the children make their way one by one up their tree chutes to begin their long journey homeward. Little do they know that the pirates were the victorious ones that day and that Hook has commanded one of his men to beat the Indian drum as a way of luring the children out of their underground lair. As they come to the surface, their mouths are quickly muffled, and they are easily taken prisoner by the gloating pirates.

All during this time, Peter is below ground thinking that Wendy, her brothers, and the lost boys have met the victorious Piccaninnies and are being led by them through the woods of Neverland on the first leg of their return home. Left alone to himself, he does not quite know what to do. He plays with his pipes for a while to show that he does not miss Wendy. To grieve her, he decides not to take his medicine (as she had ordered him to do before she left); he lies down on bed on the outside of the covers (she always tucked him in); he laughs instead of cries (to make her indignant). Before long, he grows tired of distracting himself in this way. His eyes grow heavy, and he soon falls into a deep, dreamless sleep.

Hook, in the meantime, cannot understand why he has captured all the children except for Pan. He peers down one of the tree chutes and wonders if his boyish nemesis is still down there. He soon learns that Slightly, one of the lost boys, has widened his chute to accommodate his increasing weight. Since it is now wide enough for a full-grown man to fit into, the evil pirate captain slides down it and discovers Peter innocently asleep on his bed. Hook has him in his clutches and tries to concoct a suitable way to end his life. When he sees Peter's medicine bottle, he knows just what to do. He opens it, pours five drops of a deadly poison into it, and slithers in silence back to the surface. Hook has hatched his evil plot right under Peter's nose. The boy dreams on without the slightest clue of the danger awaiting him.

Looking Deeper

The surprise attack of the pirates throws the Indians completely off guard. Following the unwritten rules of savage warfare used in Neverland, the Piccaninnies prepare themselves for every eventuality—except one. They cannot conceive of the possibility of Hook and his cronies bypassing the law (even if it is an unwritten one) and taking a different tack. Innovation by itself can bring a sense of confusion and disorientation to people's lives. When it is combined with evil, the results can be disastrous.

Hook uses innovation to defeat the Indians, but deception to bring the children into his evil clutches. His use of the tom-tom lures the children into a false sense of security and demonstrates yet another way that evil finds its way into a person's life. Hook uses a lie to bring the children out of the security of their underground home and out into the open. As with his use of innovation to defeat the Piccaninnies, this lie takes the children completely by surprise. Up until this point of the story, Peter and the lost boys have usually had the upper hand in their dealings with Hook. Now, Hook proves himself a master of innovation and deception, two powerful instruments which, when harnessed by evil intentions, wreak great havoc in the lives of the victims.

Hook's evil reach makes its way even into the underground home, that secure haven which throughout the tale is closely associated with the unconscious. Taking advantage of Slightly's whittled-out tree, he slips down into Peter's home (much like a snake), poisons Peter's medicine (with a venomous concoction), and then crawls back up on his belly to wait for Peter to take his own life. Here, innovation and deception have given way to cold, calculating savagery. Evil goes to great lengths to achieve its ends. When given the chance, it corrupts even a person's unconscious, the one area of a person's life he or she has little control over. As personified in Hook, evil has proven itself a formidable enemy. What is supposed to make Peter well is used for contrary purposes and promises to be the cause of his downfall. Evil makes its way into Peter's life without his even knowing it. Whether he takes his medicine or not is something he alone decides—or does he?

Reflection Questions

1. Have you ever been taken totally by surprise by another person or persons? If so, was it a critical situation where you had a lot to lose? How did you handle the situation? Were you able to react to it? Did the situation get out of hand?

2. What do you think about innovation? Do you actively look for new ways of doing things? Do you shy away from it? Hope it never comes? Do you think innovation is normally a harbinger of good? Of evil? A mixture of both?

3. Have you ever done something simply out of spite and in order to vex someone else? If so, did you do it with the person's knowledge or without it? What exactly did you do? What did it accomplish? How did it make you feel? Knowing what you know now, would you do it again?

4. Have you ever been deceived by another person? If so, what was the nature of the lie? Were you deceived into giving something up? Into doing something against your will? When did you discover the deception? Did it change you attitude toward the person or persons who promulgated the lie? Did it change your perception of yourself?

5. To what extent has evil touched your life? Has it poisoned your relationships? Your environment? Your body? Your emotions? Your mind? Has it penetrated your unconscious? Has it touched your spirit? How do you deal with the various presences of evil in your life?

Chapter Twelve

Believing in Fairies

Peter rises from sleep long after Hook's departure. He has barely opened his eyes when he hears a knock on his door from up above. When he learns it is Tinker Bell, he opens the door, lets her in, and learns that Hook has captured Wendy and the boys and taken them to his pirate ship. When Peter hears that Wendy is in trouble, he vows to rescue her and grabs his medicine out of a desire to please her. Tink screams not to drink it because just moments before she had heard Hook bragging to his men about his evil deed. Peter brushes her claim off as nonsense for, unaware of Slightly's secret, he insists that Hook had no way of getting down into the underground home. Tink cannot answer Peter, for even she did not know how Hook had gained access to the underground lair.

A Fairy's Death

There is now no more time for words. Peter raises his medicine to his mouth. Just as he is about to take a sip, Tink rushes between his lips and the cup and drinks it down to the dregs. Peter asks her why she drank his medicine, but Tink is staggering in the air and cannot answer. After a moment, she opens her eyes, tells him that his medicine was poisoned and that she is about to die. Peter understands that Tink drank the poison to save him. When he asks why, Tink can do nothing but flutter slowly over to him and give his chin a loving bite.

Tink then barely makes her way to her chamber, where she lies down on the bed and closes her eyes. Peter looks into her tiny room and sees her light slowly growing fainter and fainter. He hears her muttering something but can barely make it out. Peter listens harder and soon makes out what could very well be her dying words. She tells him that she thinks she might be able to get well if she knew that children believed in fairies. Upon hearing this, Peter flings his arms around the room. Since there are no children close by, he addresses all those children who might be asleep and dreaming of Neverland at that moment. They are now the children closest to him, and they are Tink's only hope.

When Peter asks them if they believe, Tink sits up to listen for the response. At first, she thinks she hears an affirmative response, but then she is not sure. She asks Peter what he thinks, and he asks all the children who are dreaming of Neverland at that moment to clap their hands if they believed. As the story goes: "Many clapped. Some didn't. A few little beasts hissed." Then, out of nowhere, the clapping suddenly stops, as mothers the world over rush into their children's nurseries to see what the ruckus is all about. By that time, however, Tink is already saved. In fact, she is already darting through the room as effervescent and cheeky as ever. She does not stop to thank those who saved her, but she would love to know how to get her hands on those who hissed. But there is no time for that at present. With Tinker Bell in the clear, it is now time to rescue Wendy.

Looking Deeper

Being capable of only one emotion at a time, Tinker Bell is capable of feats of heroism and also of great mischief. She is not an evil character, even though she manages to do some pretty nasty things throughout the story—especially to Wendy. She merely follows her nature according to the lights given to her. In the present instance, her great love for Peter propels her to intervene on his behalf. She saves Peter by drinking the poison intended for him. She, in turn, is saved by Peter's invocation of children throughout the world to proclaim their belief in her existence.

Tinker Bell's heroic action has saving, redemptive value not only for Peter, but also for herself. It brings out the best in her and reveals her true character. There is an angelic quality in Tink, one that is both attractive and repulsive. Having the potential to do either evil or good, she finds herself playing with the former (as with fire), but ultimately choosing the latter. This choice defines her existence. Even though, as later events make apparent, Peter's feeble memory eventually makes him forget all about her, her name and her being will be forever linked to his. Throughout the story, Peter is the one character who can rein Tink in and keep her from giving in to her baser instincts. It is Peter, moreover, who elicits from her her greatest potential. Tinker

Bell is a heroine in her own right. She brings an aspect of mystery to the story and reminds us that, even on the spiritual level, the struggle between good and evil wages an intense battle for survival.

Finally, Tinker Bell survives because children believe in her. This part of the story is a testament to the power of faith. Believing in someone imparts to him or her a sense of purpose and well-being that cannot be underestimated. Not everyone believes in Tink, but enough do to make a difference in her life. Without that sign of assurance, it would be all too easy for her to succumb to the poison planted by Hook in the depths of the unconscious. Such evil is overcome only by the power of faith, a gift which comes from beyond and marks the true turning point in the story.

Reflection Questions

1. Did you believe in fairies when you were a child? If so, do you recall what they were like? How did they behave? Were you enchanted by them? Afraid of them? Upset by them? Did you ever hiss at them? When did you stop believing in fairies?

2. What does it mean to believe in somebody? To stick by him or her in times of trouble? To root for him or her when everyone else has given up? To lift him or her up in times of failure? To see his or her deepest potential? To encourage him or her to be the best person he or she can possibly be?

3. Have you ever been the beneficiary of a heroic action? Who was it that saved you? Someone you knew? Someone you did not know? Someone you would have expected? Someone you never thought could have done such a thing?

4. What can faith do and not do? Can it prevent someone from dying? Can it bring someone back to life? Can it move mountains? Are there different kinds of faith? If so, how so? Is faith natural to the human heart? Unnatural to it? Supernatural? Is faith a gift? If so, who gives it—and why? If not, where does it come from?

5. Have you ever performed an act of heroism? If not, would you like to? Do you think you would be capable of it? Are there any special character traits you think you would need? Can anyone be a hero?

Chapter Thirteen

The Pirate Ship

The moon is already rising when Peter surfaces from his tree heavily armed and eager to make his way to the pirate ship where Hook and his men have taken their prisoners. He cannot take to the air because of heavy clouds, so he resolves to get there by foot. The way to proceed is not all that clear since a light snowfall has covered all footprints. Well adept at tracking and the lore of the land, he proceeds with great caution, aware that danger may be waiting for him behind every tree. He sees the crocodile crossing his path and makes his way through the forest with one finger on his lip and the other on his dagger. He scents a battle in the making and aims to be victorious.

Walking the Plank

Hook's ship, The Jolly Roger, is low in the water of Kidd's Creek near the mouth of the pirate river.

She is shrouded in darkness and has an ominous air about her. Hook has the children in the brig and is walking the deck. He is overcome with a deep sense of loneliness, a feeling that increases when he is around people. The captain, the reader is told, graduated from an elite British public school where keeping one's form was bred into him at an early age. He worries about "good form" in a compulsive manner, so much so that he even wonders if thinking about keeping it is really a sign of bad form. He cares little about the substance of his actions, just so long as they look good.

Hook orders the boys to be brought up from the brig and has the plank readied for them to walk. Their faces are deathly white. He tells them that he needs two cabin boys for the Jolly Roger and asks for volunteers. The boys decline, saying that their mothers would not approve of their being pirates. Hook then singles John and Michael out, telling them that they would make fine pirates and that they would be known respectively as Red-handed Jack and Blackbeard Joe. The boys are tempted but decline once they learn that they would have to swear to the downfall of the King of England.

Wendy is then brought up to witness her children's death. The boys gather around her to hear her last words to them. She tells them what she believes their real mothers would hope for them—that they die like English gentlemen. The boys all promise to fulfill this wish. Hook is enraged by Wendy's words and orders her tied to the mast. The moment of truth has arrived. The boys shiver in fear as they are pushed toward the plank. Hook shows his teeth and smiles as he watches their frozen stares. He steps toward Wendy to turn her face toward the boys so that she can witness their death one by one. He never gets the chance to hear Wendy's cries of anguish for, at that very moment, he hears the dreaded ticking sound of the crocodile. In an instant, Hook is transformed from a sinister pirate captain to a slobbering coward. His limbs become limp, and he is frozen in fear. He orders his men to hide him as he frantically eyes a quick means of escape. The boys, in the meantime, look over the ship's side and see that it is Peter, rather than the crocodile, who is making the ticking sound and coming to their aid. Once again, Hook has been outwitted by his Neverland nemesis.

Looking Deeper

Hook is so concerned about "good form" that he actually has none. He projects the image of being a fearless pirate captain, but it disappears the moment he hears the fateful ticking of the crocodile. Hook is a lonely, unhappy pirate. He relates to no one except through fear and intimidation. Once these weapons are taken from him, he does not know how to act or carry himself. Hook fears the awful sound of the crocodile, the ticking of time which, even in Neverland, pursues him without relent. Rather than face it courageously, he tries to hide and run away from it. Even though he knows that he cannot escape it, his only reaction to it is what lies beneath his fearless outward appearance. The crocodile reveals Hook's inward cowardly nature. It shows him to be the epitome of bad form, someone without a backbone, unable to take a stand when the odds are against him and time is running out.

The boys are physically in Hook's clutches, but that is all. They turn from his attractive offers to join his crew as cabin boys. One by one, they stand up to him, telling him things he does not understand or has forgotten about long ago. At their age, the boys find courage as a result of the strong motherly influence in their lives. They imagine their mothers would not want them to be pirates—and so they refuse. They are elated when they hear Wendy speaking to them on behalf of their real mothers and telling them to die like English gentlemen. Much to Hook's chagrin, the boys are all displaying good form. Even their fear in the face of imminent death does not dispel this impression, for one knows that, no matter what happens, each has taken Wendy's words to heart and is ready to die for them. They display good form precisely because they are not concerned about it. They care only about doing the right thing. At that age, their perception of what is right has very much to do with what their mothers tell them. Through Wendy, the boys are getting back in touch with the love that has eluded them for so long. From that moment on, they can no longer be counted among the lost.

Wendy and Peter's actions bring about Hook's unexpected demise. Wendy helps the boys to overcome their fears and to stare death in the eye. Peter, in turn, tricks Hook into revealing his own cowardly nature in front of Wendy, the boys, and his entire crew. Wendy helps the boys face a seemingly hopeless situation with courage and dignity. Peter uses innovation to outsmart Hook and take him by surprise. Imitating the crocodile's ticking sound is the perfect strategy at just the right time to reveal Hook's propensity toward cowardice and bad form. Peter has Hook right where he wants him, and the battle is just getting underway.

Reflection Questions

1. What does it mean to be concerned only with one's form? Does it mean caring only about appearances? About the impression one makes on others? Have you ever met anyone concerned solely with such things? Do you see any of yourself reflected in them?

2. What role does a person's educational background have in shaping his or her character? A great deal? Little at all? Does it depend on the individual? The institutions involved? What effect has your own schooling had on making you the person you are today? What were it advantages and disadvantages?

3. What role does a parent play in shaping a child's sense of right and wrong? A major role? A

minor role? Is that role more important than a child's own natural disposition? Is it more important than the environment in which the child is brought up? Is the mother's role different from the father's in this matter?

4. Does being courageous mean not being afraid? Not showing one's fears? Acting in a courageous manner in spite of one's fears? Do you consider yourself a courageous person? Would you like to be? What character traits do you think you would need?

5. How do you think you would act in the face of imminent death? Even when it takes you by surprise and approaches virtually unannounced? What do you think is the worse part about dying? The pain? The uncertainty of what lies beyond? Leaving your loved ones behind? Are you ready to face death? Why do you feel this way?

Chapter Fourteen

Hook or Me

Peter arrives at the ship just in time to save Wendy and the boys. The way he gets there is an ingenious boyish invention. As he is making his way through the forest, he sees the crocodile crossing his path but does not immediately avert to the fact that it is no longer ticking. When he realizes what has happened, he rightly concludes that the ticking clock inside it has run out. The idea then comes to him to imitate the crocodile's tick so that the beasts of the forest would mistake him for the reptilian clock and allow him to pass by undisturbed. This tactic allows Peter to quicken his pace considerably and to arrive at the pirate ship at just the right moment. Once there, he continues imitating the crocodile and soon realizes that it can be of tremendous help in freeing Wendy and the boys from Hook's evil clutches. The crocodile, in turn, follows Peter to the ship and, without the hindrance of the ticking clock, eagerly awaits an unsuspecting Hook in the water.

A Fight to the End

While Hook is still frozen with fear, Peter overcomes the ship's quartermaster and silently slips into the captain's cabin. Only then does he stop making the ticking sound of the crocodile. As the ensuing silence extends throughout the ship, Hook gradually regains his composure and goes back to his normal regimen of cruel and heinous behavior. A little embarrassed by his public display of cowardice, he decides to taunt his prisoners even more than before by singing and dancing along an imaginary plank. When he finishes, he asks his prisoners if they want a touch of the cat-o'nine tails before walking the plank. Hook smiles when they fall to their knees and beg him not to break out the whip. He then orders one of his men to go into the cabin to fetch it.

When the pirate enters the cabin, Peter fells him with one sweep of his blade. A blood-curdling scream reaches the ears of those on deck. Hook sends another member of the crew inside and another chilling scream erupts from the cabin. Yet another crew member is dispatched for the whip. This one decides to jump ship rather than enter the cabin and meet a terrible death. Finally, Hook himself decides to go in and fetch the whip. This time, Peter blows out his lantern and the captain comes out spooked, almost as if he has seen a ghost. To calm the fears of his crew (as well as his own), he orders the boys into the cabin, figuring that they will either kill the demon within the hold or be killed by it. Peter, in the meantime, has found the key to the manacles binding the boys. When they enter the cabin, he frees them one by one, arms them to the teeth, and then lets out a deep crow to give the impression that they too have been slain by the creature within the cabin. The pirates' panic has now reached mammoth proportions.

In the midst of the mayhem, Hook comes to the conclusion that the ship is cursed because a girl is aboard. He looks at Wendy and orders his crew to throw her overboard. Little does he know that Peter, in the meantime, has quietly left the cabin, cut Wendy loose, and taken her place by covering himself with her cloak. As the crewmen reach for him to carry out the captain's orders, he suddenly takes off his disguise and reveals himself as "Peter Pan the avenger!" Hook and the pirates are taken completely by surprise. At that moment, the boys pour out of the cabin and enter the fray of battle. Not knowing what has hit them, the frightened pirates either jump ship or meet their doom in a feeble attempt to withstand a superior force. At the end of the battle, Hook engages Peter in a heated duel. None of his sword tricks work against Pan, who is an excellent swordsman and who has been waiting a long time to settle his score with Hook. The evil captain knows he is losing the duel and now wishes only to catch Peter, at least once, in demonstration of "bad form." He succeeds in doing so by getting Peter to kick him off the ship's bulwark into the water rather than finish him with one final thrust of the sword. With that, Hook falls into the sea and the jaws of the hungry crocodile. The action is over; the battle, won. Hook and his henchmen have lost; Peter and the boys proudly take control of the Jolly Roger.

Looking Deeper

Throughout the story, Hook and his crew parallel Peter and the lost boys in a perverse manner. They are to Peter and his boys like what pepper is to salt. The tension between them is palpable. All of Neverland is affected by their ongoing struggle. Without it, Neverland would lose its sense of lurking danger and wistful adventure.

The two groups are actually inverse reflections of each other. Peter is a boy who refuses to grow up; Hook, an evil pirate captain who has not outgrown his childish ways. The pirates, too, act more like children in adult bodies. They cannot manage the havoc they find themselves in. The lost boys defeat them easily and, in the process, take a major step toward growing up. Both groups, moreover, vie for Wendy's affection. Peter and the lost boys do so by giving her their love and attention. Hook and his motley crew seek to conquer her affections by force. Wendy's preference is clear from the very start. She is proud of the behavior of her boys, from Peter down to the timid Tootles.

On another level, the ongoing battle between the two sides represents the intense struggle between good and evil that goes on in the mind of every child. That struggle is processed unconsciously in a child's dreams and lived out consciously in his or her world of pretending and make-believe. Neverland is a place where a child's conscious and unconscious struggles merge. In Hook and his crew, Peter and the lost boys battle the very persons they wish not to become. In Peter and the lost boys, Hook and his crew struggle against children they once were like but have long since lost touch with. Each side loathes yet is strangely attracted to the other. Peter and the lost boys do not want to become men but are strongly attracted to the reckless gusto of the pirate way of life. Hook and his crew simply cannot abide Peter's boyish pranks and cocky self-confidence, but secretly wish they could be as inventive and self-assured as he. Each side shirks the responsibilities of growing up either by refusing to do so (as with Peter and the lost boys) or by simply disregarding them (as with Hook and his crew). Each side also desperately wants a mother to care for them (albeit for different reasons) and looks to Wendy to realize its dreams. Wendy realizes, however, that real mothers can only be found in the real world. It is for this reason that she wants to leave

Neverland (and especially the deck of the Jolly Roger) and return home with the boys.

The defeat of Hook and his crew allows Peter and the lost boys to proceed as planned with their earlier wishes. The lost boys continue their journey with Wendy, John, and Michael to the Darling household. Despite the risks, they feel that growing up with a real mother is worth a try. Peter, however, remains firm in his decision to stay behind. He has long forgotten what his real mother was like and prefers the kind of adventures that Neverland has in store for him. For him, defeating Hook and his pirates is just another adventure—no more; no less. He sees no reason for leaving the magical shores of this make-believe island. Neverland allows him to live in the present, forget the past, and let the future take care of itself. He likes where he is and is not about to change for anyone—not even Wendy.

Reflection Questions

1. Where did you get your sense of good and evil? Was it inborn? Did it come from your parents? Your educators? Your early environment? Your early struggles? A combination of all of these?

Has your understanding of good and evil changed over time? If so, how so?

2. How would you describe your complete opposite? Does this inverse character have any redeeming qualities? If so, what are they? Do you think other people would like this character if they met him? Would you?

3. How did the struggle between good and evil manifest itself in your childhood? Can you think of any dreams where the struggle was particularly strong? Did it manifest itself in your pretending or in the games you played?

4. What is the epitome of all that you are against in life? Has it changed over time? Have you changed over time as a result of your struggle against it? Do you see anything of yourself in what you are against? Are you attracted to it in any way?

5. How does the struggle between good and evil manifest itself in your life today? How would you describe the tension? How deeply are you aware of it? Which side seems to be winning? How do you know?

Chapter Fifteen

The Return Home

The boys do not celebrate their victory over the pirates for long before Wendy realizes the lateness of the hour and has them all off to bed. They awake early the next morning and busy themselves with the strenuous chores of sailing a ship. With Peter at the helm, they all don the garb of pirates and act as his crew. He calls them the scum of Rio and the Gold Coast, the meanest crew ever to sail the seven seas. They obey all his orders to the letter but, like all good pirates, complain behind his back. All in all, they have quite a journey ahead of them. Peter has decided to bring Wendy and the boys back himself. He steers the ship toward the mainland and figures they should reach the Azores by June 21st. From there, they will save time by flying the rest of the way.

Life Back Home

All during this time, life has been dreary back at the Darling household. Mr. and Mrs. Darling no longer go out during the evening for fear that their children would return in their absence. Mrs. Darling leaves the nursery window open each night for Wendy, John, and Michael in case they show up unannounced. Mr. Darling blames himself for tying Nana up in the back yard the night the children disappeared. He punishes himself by locking himself up inside Nana's kennel and refusing to come out. He eats, drinks, and sleeps in his makeshift jailhouse. He even goes to work in it. Each morning he is carried in it to a cab, which takes him to his office and picks him up at night. All of this creates quite a spectacle in the neighborhood, and Mr. Darling gradually attracts a large following. They feel sorry for him, yet also admire him for his public display of remorse.

Each evening, Mr. Darling comes home, sticks his head out of his cage, and kisses Mrs. Darling on the cheek. They spend the evenings together talking about their children and wondering how they are. On one particular night, Mr. Darling asks his wife to play him to sleep on the nursery piano. He is such a simple soul that he could pass for a child if he could only take his baldness off. Mrs. Darling complies with his wishes but refuses to shut the nursery window to keep out the chill. She reminds him that the window must be kept open in case the children come back. Mr. Darling apologizes profusely when he realizes his mistake. Within minutes, his wife's playing has lulled him to sleep. She continues playing for a while.

While she is playing, Peter Pan and Tinker Bell enter the children's bedroom that adjoins the day nursery. He orders Tink to shut the window and make a quick getaway with him. His reason for accompanying Wendy and the boys home is now clear. By shutting the window before their arrival, he wants them to think their mother has forgotten about them and is no longer waiting for them. He dances with glee at his own cleverness. As he does so, he hears Mrs. Darling's music in the background and quietly goes over to watch her. He admires her beauty but tells Tink that she is not as beautiful as his mother (an obvious falsehood, since Peter has no recollection of his mother whatsoever). He feels sorry for her but tells Tink that he will not change his mind about the closed window. Wendy cannot be in two places at once, and Mrs. Darling simply cannot have her. As he listens to the music, however, he gets angry at Mrs. Darling for not seeing why she cannot have Wendy. As the music continues, he shifts his weight and begins to break down. Mrs. Darling's charm wins in the end—and she doesn't even know it. Peter and Tink open the window and fly out of the house.

Minutes later Wendy, John, and Michael fly into their nursery bedroom. They see Mr. Darling fast asleep in Nana's kennel and wonder why his habits have changed so. They then hear Mrs. Darling playing the music and, rather than surprise her, decide simply to slip into bed and await her discovery of them. When Mrs. Darling first sees them, she thinks she is dreaming. When she finally realizes that her children have finally come home, she is overcome with emotion. She wakes up her husband to share her joy. Nana comes rushing in to join in the happiness. Once again, all is well in the Darling household.

Looking Deeper

Without its children, the Darling household is simply miserable. Mrs. Darling worries about her children and always has an eye on the nursery window. Mr. Darling blames himself for their departure and imprisons himself for his stupidity (and in a dog kennel, no less!). This self-imposed exile attracts a considerable amount of notice and is the source of both admiration and ridicule. Most of the neighborhood children cheer him on, even a couple of adults. Liza the maid sneers at his odd behavior. Mrs. Darling tries to ease his pain. Nana has nothing to say even though she is the one he has sinned against the most.

Mr. Darling's behavior highlights the way people can imprison themselves for all sorts of very personal (and not so personal) reasons. The kennel is a portable prison, which Mr. Darling places himself in and takes with him wherever he goes. On one level, the absurdity of his predicament brings out the irrational grounds of all such self-imposed exiles. Mr. Darling, who prides himself on his ability to calculate every contingency, lacks the ability to see what he is doing to himself. As someone very concerned with public opinion, he also fails to see the ridiculous nature of a grown man living in a kennel. On another level. Mr. Darling is simply doing to himself in a very visible way what many other people do to themselves emotionally on a daily basis. His prison is visible; most other people erect and place themselves in invisible prisons as a result of the shame they carry around with them.

The open nursery window is a symbol of hope for the Darling household. It must remain open; otherwise, there will be no way for the Darling children to reenter their home. This attitude of openness is essential for the health of a family. By closing the window, Peter shows that he is capable of great cruelty. The power of Mrs. Darling's motherly concern, however, reveals the deepest inclinations of his heart and his inability to carry out his plan. As much as he would hate to admit, the care of a real mother for her children still has a hold over him. Peter, however, is out the window before he even has a chance to realize this. At the reunion of the Darling family, he finds himself on the outside of the nursery window looking in. By choosing to return to Neverland, he bars himself from life in a happy home and the joy of a mother's and father's love.

Reflection Questions

1. In what ways have you imprisoned yourself during your life? What were the surface reasons for it? The deeper ones? Did it involve your ideas? Your emotions? Your relationships with others? With God? Were you able to get out of your self-inflicted imprisonment? Are you still in it?

2. Have you ever missed someone you loved? What does it feel like? How would you best describe the emotion? Have you ever shared that feeling with the person you missed? If not, why not?

3. What is it like waiting for the return of someone you miss very much? Is it worse if you do not know exactly when they are coming? How do you spend your time waiting for them? Did you ever get the feeling they would never come back?

4. What windows have you left open in your life for other people? Your mind? Your heart? Your emotions? Your availability? Do others perceive

you as approachable? Do your loved ones perceive you that way? Have you ever shut the window of your heart on someone? Why did you do so? How did they react?

5. Have you ever been reunited after a long time apart with someone for whom you care a great deal? What was the experience like? What thoughts passed through your mind? What feelings did you feel? Did you ever experience your family in this way? What, in your mind, is the greatest joy a person can experience in life? The greatest sorrow? Are the two in any way connected?

Chapter Sixteen

When Wendy Grows Up

While the Darling children are being reunited with their family, the lost boys stay below to give Wendy time to explain their situation. After counting to five hundred, they cannot wait any longer. They march upstairs and stand in a row in front of Wendy's mother. Their eyes ask her to have them. Mrs. Darling immediately says she would be happy to be their mother. Mr. Darling is a bit daunted by an additional six mouths to feed but is easily persuaded by Wendy and her mother. The boys are ecstatic at their newfound home—all but Peter, that is. He flies by the window one more time to say good-bye to Wendy. Wendy's mother sees him and offers to be his mother as well. When he finds out that she would send him to school and that he would have to go to the office and become a man, he outright refuses. He tells Wendy that the fairies placed the house he and the lost boys had built for her high in the treetops and that he and Tinker Bell are going to live in it. Before he leaves, he receives permission from Mrs. Darling to have Wendy visit him for spring cleaning in Neverland once a year for a whole week. With that, he flies off and makes his way back to the magic island.

Spring Cleaning

Life eventually goes back to normal at the Darling household. The boys are sent off to school and soon realize what a mistake they had made in not wanting to remain in Neverland. Their decision is irrevocable, however, and they soon settle down to the ordinary life of British school children. One sad effect of their new lifestyle, however, is that they gradually forget how to fly. At first, Nana ties their feet down at night so they will not fly away. In time, they find that they cannot let themselves down lightly off the school bus or even fly after their hats on a windy day. Before long, they cease believing in Neverland altogether and do not wish to fly any-more. Michael, the youngest of the group, believes longer than the others and is ridiculed for it.

Peter keeps his promise and returns for Wendy at the end of the first year. She is already outgrowing the frock of leaves and berries she had made in Neverland. Peter does not notice, however, for he is too busy thinking about himself. Much to Wendy's surprise, he has completely forgotten about Captain Hook and even Tinker Bell. He says he has too many adventures to remember them all and that he suspects Tink is dead (fairies generally do not live very long, the narrator tells us). Peter does not come for Wendy the following year, and Michael delicately asks Wendy if such a person ever existed. When he comes the following year to take Wendy away for Spring cleaning, Peter is not aware at all that he has missed a year. That is the last time that Wendy sees him as a little girl.

Years pass. The boys have all grown up and have long forgotten their exploits with Peter. Wendy is married with a little girl of her own. She has long forgotten how to fly, and Peter is all but a faded memory. Her daughter Jane, however, dreams about Neverland and sometimes hears Peter's crowing in her dreams. Wendy tells her that as a little girl she used to hear him while she was awake. Jane tells her how lucky she was and begs her to tell her more of her early adventures. Once a week, on the nurse's night off, she tells Jane stories of Neverland and of the wonderful things that happened to her flying at Peter's side. To heighten the sense of adventure, she and her daughter often pull the bed sheets over themselves in the shape of a tent.

On one particular night, Jane has fallen asleep, and Wendy is sitting on the floor close to the fire in order to see the clothes she is mending. Out of nowhere, Peter flies through the window and greets her. He is as boyish as ever and still with his first set of teeth. Wendy is embarrassed for having grown up and become an adult. In the dimly lit room, Peter does not see any change in her at first. When Wendy finds the courage to tell him that she is now a married woman with a child as her own, he steps back in disbelief, verifies what she has told him with his own eyes, then falls to the floor and begins to cry. Wendy rushes out of the room to gather her thoughts and think of what to do. In the meantime, Peter's crying has awakened Jane, who recognizes him immediately and tells him that she has been waiting for him for a long time. Wendy returns to the room to find Peter sitting on Jane's bedpost crowing to his heart's content. Peter turns to Wendy and tells her that Jane is his mother. Before long, Jane is flying about the room at Peter's side and sets out with him for Neverland to help him with spring cleaning. And so, the adventure continues with Wendy's daughter Jane, and later with Jane's daughter Margaret, and with her daughter, and so on. The story ends saying this will go on, "so long as children are gay and innocent and heartless."

Looking Deeper

It does not take long for the lost boys to lose touch with Neverland. First, they forget how to fly and then they lose their faith in the existence of the magic island. Before long, Peter is nothing but a distant memory. After their first week of school, they have regrets about the land of adventure they have left behind. Within a short while, however, their daily routine of life has numbed their imaginations and weakened their grasp over their dreams of childhood. The lost boys have been found at tremendous cost. They have emerged from a land of the eternal present to a place where time moves forward at a predictable rate. As they grow old, their memories of Neverland recede to the background. In the adults they eventually become, one can hardly recognize the children they once were.

Peter is the perennial child. Within the space of a year, he has long forgotten Hook and Tinker Bell. He comes back to visit Wendy once, then two years later, and one more time many years after that (so much for his promise of a yearly visit). He throws a tantrum when he realizes that Wendy has grown up, but his attention is quickly diverted by Wendy's daughter. Like any child, Peter lives only in the present, thinks only about himself, and says the first thing that comes into his head. He is incredibly loveable, however, as Wendy has learned—and many other children after her. He cannot be held accountable for his tendency to forget. He is only a child after all. He represents the magic of childhood, that part of life which every person must pass through, but which too many people unfortunately lose touch with. Although some manage to carry a bit of it with them through life, most adults are no longer acquainted with the children they once were so very long ago. By losing touch with this important aspect of their past, something is often missing in their sense of self-identity and affects the way they live in the present and orient themselves toward the future.

When Wendy meets Peter at the end of the story, she is at first a little ashamed of herself. As she tries to conceal her adult body from Peter, the little child within her cries out to be let free. She eventually regains her composure and reveals herself to him as she truly is. She knows that she cannot turn back the clock, and she finds that she now looks at Peter in a different way. She no longer has a girlish crush on him, but looks at him with motherly care and affection, the way Mrs. Darling had looked upon him so many years ago. Wendy appreciates Peter as an important part of her childhood. Without him, she would never have become the person she now is. She recognizes the role he has played in her life and welcomes the role he will play in her daughter's life. Wendy remembers the little girl she once was and, to some extent, still is. She cannot fly, but she remembers that she once did. She can no longer return to Neverland, but she has stories to tell her daughter and has told them so well and so many times that her daughter now knows them better than she. Wendy has been to Neverland and survived to tell other children about it. She has mothered the lost boys and has become a better mother in real life because of it. She is hesitant and full of motherly concern as she watches her daughter fly off with Peter. At the same time, she remembers what her journey meant to her and knows that Jane's journey to Neverland will help her get in touch with her deepest dreams. The hardest part, she now knows, is for a person to stay in touch with these dreams and to keep them alive at every point in his or her journey through life. Wendy has grown up, but she has not forgotten her exploits with Peter in Neverland. He has made a difference in her adult life without her (or him) even knowing it. Wendy has grown up but taken much of her childhood past with her. For that, there is much to rejoice in and be thankful for.

Reflection Questions

1. Is there a part of you that regrets having grown up? Is it a large part? A medium-sized part? A very small part? Do you know why you feel that way? Is something from your childhood missing from your life? Can you put your finger on what it might be?

2. Did you view time differently as a child than as an adult? Can you describe the difference?

Which perception of time do you prefer? The child's? The adult's? A mixture of both? Why?

3. Have you ever felt as though a little boy or girl was crying out inside of you begging to be let free? Do you feel that way a lot? Once in a while? Hardly at all? What do you think such feelings are trying to tell you?

4. Have you lost touch with the child you once were and, to a large extent, still are? If so, what makes you feel that way? How does it manifest itself in your life? Do you wish to get in touch with that lost little boy or girl? What can you do to make things better?

5. Do you think it is possible to be a responsible adult and also child-like? If so, what child-like qualities would you like to nurture in your life? How would you go about nurturing them? What should you try to avoid?

Wendy

For a little longer
she tried
for his sake
not
to have
growing pains;

and
she felt
she was
untrue
to him
when
she got
a prize
for
general knowledge.

but
the years
came
and went
without
bringing
the careless boy;

and
when
they met
again
Wendy was

A married woman.[3]

---

[3] Ibid., 162. [Poetically arranged]

www.ingramcontent.com/pod-product-compliance
Lightning Source LLC
Chambersburg PA
CBHW052106090426
42741CB00009B/1703